THE MOON IS ABOUT
238,855 MILES AWAY

THE MOON IS ABOUT 238,855 MILES AWAY

MARTIN STANNARD

All rights reserved. No part of this work covered by the copyright herein may be reproduced or used in any means—graphic, electronic, or mechanical, including copying, recording, taping, or information storage and retrieval systems—without written permission of the publisher.

Printed by imprintdigital
Upton Pyne, Exeter
www.digital.imprint.co.uk

Typesetting and cover design by narrator
www.narrator.me.uk
info@narrator.me.uk
033 022 300 39

Published by Shoestring Press
19 Devonshire Avenue, Beeston, Nottingham, NG9 1BS
(0115) 925 1827
www.shoestringpress.co.uk

First published 2019
© Copyright: Martin Stannard (www.martinstannard.com)
© Cover image: "untitled" (lithographic ink on paper, 42x30cm, 2018) by Dale Devereux Barker (www.daledevereuxbarker.co.uk)

The moral right of the author has been asserted.

ISBN 978-1-912524-43-3

ACKNOWLEDGMENTS

Some of these poems have appeared (sometimes in slightly different form) in the following journals:

Litter: Fishing, Alive, Reading at Sunrise, Waiting At South Pavilion, A Farewell (Wáng Wéi)

Meniscus: In Late Autumn, The Sandpiper, A Message in Autumn, Visiting an Old Friend, Oranges

Tears in the Fence: Lament #4, Looking at the Moon, The Moon Is About 238,855 Miles Away, Retirement

A NOTE TO THE POEMS

The originals of the poems here are from the Tang dynasty (618–907), a time generally regarded as the great period of classical Chinese poetry. These versions are just that: versions, and not direct translations, hence the "after…." at the beginning of their attributions.

My process has been to create a direct translation, and then rework the poem to some degree, a degree that varies depending upon the individual poem. In some cases I have removed names and/or places, or Chinese idioms or cultural references that either do not usefully translate or that would be meaningless to a reader without the necessary knowledge of Chinese culture. In some cases I have moved things around quite a lot, and in most cases I have also slipped in a phrase or line of my own. Sometimes titles have been changed. In every case I have attempted to create a poem that is able to stand alone, rendered in the English I use in my everyday life and in my own poetry, but which stays as faithful as I know how to the meaning, tone and mood of the original. I am no Sinologist, and purists may object, but so it goes.

It is worth noting too, I think, that from living and working in China for twelve years I came to learn that many (if not most) of today's Chinese readers do not fully understand all the subtle references and allusions in China's classical poems, a fact that has given me the confidence to leave some things out. My ultimate aim has been to make poems that give pleasure and food for thought. One can only try.

Martin Stannard
April 2019

CONTENTS

A Farewell	1
The Old Fisherman	2
Fishing	3
In Early Spring	4
In Late Autumn	5
Perseverance and Hope	6
The Sandpiper	7
Thinking of a Friend at the Time of the Full Moon	8
Meeting in the Capital	9
A Message in Autumn	10
A Yellow River of Flowers	11
Alive	12
Another Day	13
Lament #4	14
Living by the Creek	15
Lodging for the Night	16
Reading at Sunrise	17
Visiting an Old Friend	18
A Letter	19
Well	20
Zither	21
Four Seasons	22
A Farewell in the Snow	23
Oranges	24
The Sword Dance	25
To a Student	26
Song for a Friend	27
At the Border	28
From the Pagoda	29
Outside Town	30
Two Songs	31
Waiting	32
Dreaming #1	33
Dreaming #2	34
At South Pavilion	35
Looking at the Moon	36

Long Forever #1	37
Long Forever #2	38
The Moon Is About 238,855 Miles Away	39
A Letter	40
From a Tower	41
Mountain Stones	42
Mooring at Dusk	43
Returning to Lumen Mountain	44
Retirement	45
The Hard Road	46
On Parting #1	47
On Parting #2	48
A Farewell	49

A FAREWELL

after 宣州谢朓楼饯别校书叔云 by Lǐ Bái

Yesterday is past
Today my heart is confused
I have many worries

The wild geese fly for miles with the wind
It's what they do and have always done
I pour more wine and watch them from my window
When I write I try to fly like that

I cut water with a knife and still it flows
So I drink to drown my worries

I cannot fly like the geese
Too often my writing does not satisfy me
Tomorrow I shall leave this place
Change is necessary

THE OLD FISHERMAN
after 渔翁 by Liù Zōngyuán

I did not sleep well
I light the morning fire
Take clear water from the river to make tea
I don't sleep well these days

Overhead
Light clouds chase one another across the sky
As far as the eye can see

I don't see well these days
It's alright to be alone
With your thoughts

FISHING

    after 春泛若耶溪 by Qíwú Qián

Thinking is as solitary as writing
I foresee no end to either
This evening my boat and I follow the current
It leads us by a path of flowers
As night deepens the stars shine above the mountains
The moon is sinking toward the treetops
Mist hangs over the surface of the water
The air is thick with all that life could turn out to be
But since it cannot be known it's not worth thinking about
So I am content
An old man fishing on my own beyond the world

IN EARLY SPRING
after 和晋陵路丞早春游望 by Dù Shěnyán

Light white clouds
The flowering plum
Willows at the ferry crossing
The yellow bird darting through warming air

Everyone is delighted
By the arrival of Spring
Clear and fine

Suddenly an old song reminds me of home

IN LATE AUTUMN

after 寄全椒山中道士 by Wéi Yingwù

The hermit priest collects kindling on the mountain
He will dine on a few potatoes by a small fire

I would take wine to him
So he might better endure

But where fallen leaves carpet the earth
I would not know how to find him

It's so cold in here as I write this

PERSEVERANCE AND HOPE
after 题大庾岭北驿 by Sòng Zhīwèn

The wild geese fly South
Only so far, then stop

At a certain time
They return to the North

When will I be able to go home?

The river is still
The forest lost in the mists at twilight

In the morning
If from this mountain I could see home
It would be to gaze upon plum blossoms
White against the snow

THE SANDPIPER
after 旅夜书怀 by Dù Fŭ

There is the lightest of breezes, and I am adrift
Under the stars, the river full of the full moon
But everything has been moving too fast for me

Poetry did not bring fame, but old age is bringing
A slowing down and over there on the mud
Is a bird, scavenging for food, trying to stay alive

THINKING OF A FRIEND AT THE TIME OF THE FULL MOON

after 同从弟南斋玩月忆山阴崔少府 by Wáng Chānglíng

I draw back the curtains in my room to reveal the full moon
Passing of time fills the emptiness
Mild moonlight bathes the river and the trees
It flows up to my door, and would flow through the window
To make the old new again

My friend is many miles away living by a different river
Tonight he will be singing songs of sadness
On the breeze the fragrance of orchids drifts

MEETING IN THE CAPITAL

after 长安遇冯著 by Wéi Yingwù

Spring flowers, young swallows nesting—
But our hair is now grey silken thread

Your clothes are damp with mountain rain
And when I ask why you have come
You say it's to buy a good axe for chopping firewood

Tomorrow you will leave—Soon it will be Spring again

A MESSAGE IN AUTUMN
after 秋登兰山寄张五 by Mèng Hàorán

I think about you up there in the mountains to the North
Secluded and at peace, thoughts floating with the white clouds

Here, people are returning home after the day's work
I can see some of them resting on the sand waiting for the ferry

Evening and encroaching darkness may bring melancholy, as
    can Autumn
I'm unsettled, my head is away, flying with the wild geese

From the riverbank I can see an island floating on the water
    like the moon
Please, like the moon, come and drink wine with me

A YELLOW RIVER OF FLOWERS
after 青溪 by Wáng Wéi

There has been some talk of a yellow river of flowers
To reach it entails following a stream of green twists and turns—
It feels, they say, like a hundred miles, but it's actually much less

They say at one point the waters crash foaming against rocks
(Here it would perhaps be more accurate to call the stream a
    torrent)
But then comes a calm of lilies and reeds, and on each bank are
Pine trees, through the branches of which the day's light is filtered

The heart, after so much journeying, also becomes calm there,
And one can imagine remaining by that river forever, forever fishing,
While not wanting, deep down, to catch anything at all

ALIVE
after 感遇#1 by Zhāng Jiǔlíng

In Spring the orchid, in Autumn the cinnamon
There is the happy life, there life is like a holiday

And when I leave to live quietly there
Where the fragrance of flowers drifts upon the breeze
And the word "alive" is a butterfly always before my eyes
Don't expect me to come back soon

Why on earth would I hurry from there back to here?

ANOTHER DAY

    after the final lines (最后几行) of 谒衡岳庙遂宿岳寺题门楼
    by Hán Yù

The moon and stars appear intermittently
From behind drifting clouds

Night slowly turns into dawn

Forced by circumstance to live alone
I have by nature never been much interested in holding high office
Or in the pleasures of the flesh
Some might describe me as a lucky man, others might not

A distant bell tolls
The sun rises cold and bright in the East
Another day for which to be thankful

LAMENT #4

    after 感遇其四 by Zhāng Jiǔlíng

Here, south of the river,
Fields of tangerine survive the Winter
They find warmth from somewhere
Even as I discover the disappointments age brings

You and your guests are happy enough
In the sun and enjoying peach trees and plum trees

Fate is chance
To speak is too often of no avail
Some people seem to float through life
One does not turn to them to enquire about the depths

Here, south of the river, fields of tangerine
And I see the Winter through

LIVING BY THE CREEK
after 溪居 by Liǔ Zōngyuán

I had been too long in the government office
And am thankful to have been exiled to the South
Where my neighbours are farmers
And I am the guest of mountain and forest

At daybreak I am turning over the earth and random thoughts
Most days I meet nobody
At night I listen to the music of the water of the creek
Tumbling over rocks, singing to the sky

LODGING FOR THE NIGHT

after 宿王昌龄隐居 by Cháng Jiàn

The moon rises clear and bright beyond the pines
And shines upon your seclusion

The creek is clear, its depth impossible to measure
As it runs by your retreat in a picture of flowers

The white clouds are your only neighbours
And a carpet of moss covers the courtyard stones

Thank you for letting me lodge here for the night
Before I go look for the birds of myth

READING AT SUNRISE
after 辰诣超师院读禅经 by Liŭ Zōngyuán

At sunrise the pines are bathed in fog and drip with dew
Bamboo in the courtyard has taken on the colour of moss

I draw water from the well
Clean my teeth and dust myself down
I read from scripture as I walk

I've been too long in darkness and want to rewrite what
    I think I am
But it's all I can do to read quietly to myself

VISITING AN OLD FRIEND
after 过故人庄 by Mèng Hàorán

At your house we dined on chicken
With greens from your garden
Then sat gazing at the green hills
Beyond the hedgerows, drinking wine

The world of other people was forgotten as we talked
And shared what has always interested us

Now I sit alone drinking chrysanthemum tea
Trying to forget and trying to remember

I shall visit you again
Wait for me

A LETTER
after 长干行 by Lǐ Bái

When we were children we were neighbours
You would come riding by on your bamboo horse
While I was picking flowers at our front door

When I was fourteen we married
My hair was cut child-like, I had that little girl's fringe
I was more than shy—I would seek out dark corners
And refuse to answer when you called

At fifteen I became more open, and soon I was all smiles
I looked to you as one might look at the full moon
It was my desire to be where you were
I was always looking for you and to you

In May your work took you away
I had just turned sixteen
And suddenly I could not touch you or talk to you

In August butterflies came, flying in pairs
Your footprints were still in the dust at the door
Now Autumn winds have covered them with dry leaves
Beside turbulent waters monkeys are crying their sorrowful cries
The butterflies have disappeared—my injured heart remains

I know sooner or later you will come home
When you do I will be at the crossroads to meet you
Until then I am sand at the mercy of the wind

WELL
after 烈女操 by Mèng Jiāo

The water in the well is never changing
A promise was made and will be kept
My love for you is the water in the well

ZITHER

    after 琴歌 by Lǐ Qí

Moon paints city walls white
Crows roost in frosty trees
Candlelight flickers on copper

The zither is clear as water
The tune is for an emperor's woman
The only sound the plucked strings
The stars are listening

I am thinking about a thousand miles away
Mountains and clouds, and you are there
All I can do is think about it because I cannot go

The song of the zither ends
You inhabit the silence

FOUR SEASONS
after 夜四時歌 by Lǐ Bái

1. Spring

The lady's white hands pick mulberry leaves
Beside crystal-clear waters
Her gown is the colour of Nature
I desire to linger here

'My silkworms are hungry. I, your servant, desire that you do not linger here.'

2. Summer

The lake is a mirror stretching for miles
The lady is gathering lotus blossoms
Before the month is out
She will have sailed away on the mirror

The moon waxes and wanes again and again

3. Autumn

The city is bathed in moonlight
The wind winds between buildings
My thoughts are blown toward the lady
Across the distance that divides us

I do not know if calm is possible

4. Winter

The lady works through the night
Sewing a shirt with her cold needle
She must finish by morning
If she is to send it with the messenger

How many days must pass until she herself can come?

A FAREWELL IN THE SNOW

after 白雪歌送武判官归京 by Cén Shēn

Snow smothers the grass
A sea of snow
Flags frozen in the north wind
Nothing can keep out the cold and damp

As dusk falls the day falls colder
Fox fur can't keep us warm
We drink to see off our friend
Fiddle and flute play as he rides away from the East Gate

Before long there is nothing to see
But the tracks of his horse in the snow
They will disappear when blossoms bless the trees
And open for the sun
But we don't forget friends

ORANGES

    after 感遇（其二）by Zhāng Jiǔlíng

Here in the sunny South
I am like the sweetest of oranges among the orange trees

Season to season year after year
I have my share of disappointment and joy

But even in Winter I find a warmth that sustains me
Until the arrival of Spring

You may occasionally invite me to enjoy the company of your
    beautiful friends
And I don't mind that, but actually I don't really think very
    much about it at all

We each have our life, our fate and fortune
The world goes on anyway

And while you play as you please
Among the peach trees and the plum trees

I'm here in the sunny South
The best of oranges among the sweet orange trees

THE SWORD DANCE
after 观公孙大娘弟子舞剑器行并序 by Dù Fŭ

The past, a beautiful girl dancing the Dance of Swords
I remember her sending silken arrows towards the moon
I remember her soaring skyward on fiery dragon wings
The sound of thunder, the silence of cloud
Red lips and imagined kisses, pearls upon her sleeves
I was alone in my head, watching the Dance of Swords

The past, disappeared into the mists where memory wanders
But I remember the warming glow of her beauty in the cold light
Many moons have come and gone, I am a man with a head of grey
Wandering the mountains with the fear of what old age holds

TO A STUDENT

    after 送綦毋潜落第还乡 by Wáng Wéi

This is hardly the most holy
Or even close to being the best of times
Even if it were
Running away is not a good choice however tempted you
    might be

So you failed the exam
And can't go to work on the mountain with the gods
That doesn't mean you have to give up and chew grass
The balance of your days

You might feel like grubbing about by a grey river
Or sitting scrunched up on a side-street in the capital
Mending old clothes for pennies
But you should do neither

Buy a flagon of wine and drink it all
Then row downriver (using your oar of laurel limb!)
And head on home

So what if today you feel forlorn like a loser
And lonely in a lonely world?
There is still a life to live
And here you know you are always among friends

SONG FOR A FRIEND

    after 送陈章甫 by Lǐ Qí

You of the noble heart
You of the dragon beard
You of the tiger brow
You of the belly full of books

April, a southerly wind, the yellow barley blowing
Blossom not yet fallen from the trees
Sunset, and the green hills you left this morning can still be seen

Dusk, and travellers are stranded for the night
When it's too dark for the ferry to cross

You of the noble heart
You who refuse to bow your head
You with numerous friends
You with numerous acquaintances

You who cannot see the full moon in the high clouds
Because you drank yourself blind at the East Gate
You who were dismissed from office yesterday

Count the friends and acquaintances you had then
Count how many you have today

AT THE BORDER

    after two poems by Wáng Chānglíng

1. 塞下曲

I let my horse drink while I think of my lady's beautiful eyes
The limpid autumn waters are cold—Wind cuts like a cutlass

The day is not yet over but we are in a place deep and dark

In former days there were battles here
Everyone speaks of great honour and courage

Yellow reeds and yellow grass grow above bones in the sand

2. 塞上曲

It's cold—The mountain pass is desolate
The din of cicadas comes from leafless mulberry trees
Yellow reeds and yellow grass are everywhere

Soldiers are buried in the sand near here

Never mind their esteem and their bays
You don't want to envy all of that
You don't want to be bones in the sand

FROM THE PAGODA
after 与高适薛据登慈恩寺浮图 by Cén Shēn

It's a clever work, almost unearthly
Its four sides absorb the sun
It's as if we might touch the sky

From the highest platform
We look down at birds
A little alarmed by the voice of the wind

Survey the world—
The mountains are a wave of rock headed East, imperious
Green pagoda trees line the main road to the South
The palace shines, it's made of jewellery
In the West are the colours of Autumn
An ash grey valley of graves lies to the North

Give me my hat—
In every direction there is something worth knowing
Today I'm going North

OUTSIDE TOWN

    after 东郊 by Wéi Yingwù

Cooped up in the office month after month
It's a relief to get away a while among the willows
To relax in the quiet of green hills
There is bird song from somewhere
Even endless light rain can't spoil this

One day work will be over and done with
And I would build a house here—
But I know many people have a similar dream

TWO SONGS

after 八月十五夜赠张功曹 by Hán Yù

1.

When I leave my bed I fear snakes
When I eat or drink I fear poisons

The air smells of decay

People are promoted ahead of me
Criminals are released on to the streets

Corruption is swept under the carpet

When I return to my hometown
It's full of bullies and thugs

2.

Your singing voice is sick at heart
I can't listen, it's too much

Stop! I say—Listen to this song instead:

Look at the moon—how bright it is tonight

Our time on earth is neither correct nor incorrect
So uncork that bottle, be like the moon

WAITING
after 宿业师山房待丁大不至 by Mèng Hàorán

The moonlight falling through the branches of the trees
Brings with it the chill of evening
The valley is a shadow now the sun has set behind the mountain
I hear the spring running clear

The birds are roosting in the branches of the trees
The woodcutters have gone home
For every creature it's the closing down of the day
And here I am, working my way through a bottle of wine
Waiting for you because you said you would come

DREAMING #1

    after 梦李白之一 by Dù Fŭ

Life is full of separations and sorrows
And partings brought about by death usually bring tears

You are always in my heart but there has been no news from you
So far away down in the south where breathing can kill you

Last night I dreamed of you
I dreamed of you trapped like a bird in a net

I feared for your safety
I feared you would never again be free to be with me

Then, as is the way of dreams, you came to me
From out of a forest, flying from the shadows

Your whole life has been one long journey of the soul
Along a very long road I cannot begin to imagine

The gentle light of the full moon illuminates my room
And there are oceans to cross, unknown dangers to face

DREAMING #2
after 梦李白之二 by Dù Fǔ

Clouds drift
Some people drift like clouds
Some people go away like clouds and never return

I dreamed you last night
We were smoking and drinking
And talking about men we've loathed and girls we've loved
And you said you feel like a boat tossed on stormy waters

Well, the world is full of people
To whom we are just old men with white hair
Who drink too much and complain too much

Well, for all their wealth and power, they will soon be forgotten
And the world will still be talking about us in a thousand years

Another thing I know for sure: friends often go away
To lose themselves in this world or find themselves in the next

I want to dream you again tonight
Coming through the door clutching a bottle of wine

AT SOUTH PAVILION
after 夏日南亭怀辛大 by Mèng Hàorán

In the West the sun has slipped down behind the mountain
And to enjoy the cool of the evening I untie my hair
And throw the windows open wide

The moonlight lies upon East Lake
And the scent of lotus blossom fills the air
And dew drips from bamboo

Night birds cry
And I want to make something too: music, or a few lines of poetry

But you're not here to enjoy any of this with me
And all I have is the consolation of whatever I can dream

LOOKING AT THE MOON
    after 月夜 by Dù Fǔ

I imagine you shivering alone in your room
Looking out the window at the moon

You are far away in the capital
But distance does not separate us

I imagine the fragrance of your hair
And remember the jade bracelet upon your arm

You know I will look at the same moon
Until I come to clear your tears away with my kisses

LONG FOREVER #1

    after 长相思之一 by Lǐ Bái

Autumn lassitude—Golden leaves falling—
A light frost
    Cold and dismal
    Inconsolable I weep
    My lantern dark under the full moon
Beauty flowers far away—
The endless heavens—
What it's like to miss someone—
Long forever

LONG FOREVER #2
after 长相思之二 by Lǐ Bái

The music is stopped, the instruments put away
You could not hear my song—It was for you
I wish the Spring wind could have taken it to you

The colour has gone out of the day
The flowers are lost in the evening mist

Do you remember my eyes?
They were once girlishly bright
Now they are full of a woman's tears
I am too miserable to sleep

If you don't believe me come and see me
Come and see how my mirror reflects only sadness—
Long forever

THE MOON IS ABOUT 238,855 MILES AWAY
after 望月怀远 by Zhāng Jiǔlíng

I see the sea illumined by the full moon
You are far away, I long to share what I see
Moonlight floods the sea, I miss you

I turn out my light
Moonlight floods the room
I am all at sea without you I am cold
Even in the warmest clothes I am cold

You are far away, I long to share this light
I go to bed but can't sleep
I am full of you, the moon and great distances

A LETTER

    after 寄韩谏议 by Dù Fǔ

Today is without music
I would come to you but lie sick in bed
Separated from all beauty

Today is without beauty
I can only imagine geese on the wing
Young leaves turning red
Cold sky hinting of frost to come

In the capital crowds flock to their gods
Lords and ladies in the star palace
Cavalrymen pose astride phoenix and unicorn
Banners of lotus leaves fluttering as mist falls
Reflections in river water of people not really there
A past still present but now wretched

The country is without music and beauty
But how can I say this?
Even as it falls apart I sense the sweet smell of the maple

When one is old there is a choice—
Life in the capital, in office,
The paying of tribute

Or to lie beside limpid waters
The eyes of a girl

FROM A TOWER

    after 登幽州台歌 by Chén Ziáng

Heaven and earth go on and on
But the wise men of old are gone

I don't see their equivalent here now
I don't see their equivalent coming

Melancholy

        Alone

                Don't cry

MOUNTAIN STONES
after 山石 by Hán Yù

The mountain does not move, the path is constant
At the temple bats fly at dusk
New rain shines
On white flowers and dark green leaves

After rice and soup
The monk prepares a bed for me
The night falls deep and calm
Mountains illuminated, the clarity of a full moon

Leaving at dawn, I temporarily lose my way
In the mist among pines and oaks
Crossing meandering streams I walk
Barefoot on stones, the wind getting up

It occurs to me this is the best way to live life
Not hemmed in by others
I may stay here
All I need is two or three friends and the world

MOORING AT DUSK
    after 夕次盱眙县 by Wéi Yingwù

I lowered the sails, the harbour was quiet
Workers were heading home

The weather was worsening, the wind rose
Rain fell as darkness fell

I remember when I lived in the mountains
And all the nights I could not sleep

RETURNING TO LUMEN MOUNTAIN
after 夜归鹿门山歌 by Mèng Hàorán

At dusk the temple bell sounds
From the ferry the clamour of people eager to be home
Others trudge the sand toward the village

I take a boat to Lumen Mountain
Moon shines and pines stand in smoky light
Lining the desolate footpath

This place is so hidden, so concealed
Only a remote and secluded man
Would choose to live in this secluded and remote place

RETIREMENT

    after 輞川閑居 by Wáng Wéi

Since coming here, since accepting I am no longer young
Since coming here to live in a world of tree and sky
Where still waters reflect leaf and cloud
Birds fly over the mountains in silence
Far from the world of my past life
I draw from the well, water the vegetables, and eat alone

THE HARD ROAD
    after 行路难之一 by Lǐ Bái

I have little coin
Food and wine is expensive
So I don't feel like eating or drinking
And cast aside dish and glass

I'm looking around
I'm seeing nothing
I'm feeling empty

I'd cross the river to get away but the ferry is iced in
I'd climb the mountain but snow has closed the door to the sky

The road's hard, travel is difficult
There are many turnings, distractions to right and left
I could be ambitious
Sometimes I am but usually I'm not

But now I'm dreaming of sailing to the sun
I am sailing to the sun
I am the sun

ON PARTING #1

after 金陵酒肆留別 by Lǐ Bái

Blowing in from the river bank
The fragrance of willow blossom
Fills the air

My friends are here to see me off
We drain our glasses
I don't really want to leave
They don't really want me to go

Which is longer—the river
Or the time this sadness will last?

ON PARTING #2
after 初发扬子寄元大校书 by Wéi Yingwù

To part is to float off into the fog, cold and dismal—
But Time with its cruelty will have its way
And I must return home

We may never see each other again

To be adrift in this world is to be in this world—
Or am I safe on these waters, even without you?

A FAREWELL
after 送别 by Wáng Wéi

I dismount, tie up the horse
And we settle down with some wine
And I ask where you are going, and why

You say you no longer feel at home here
And will return to South Mountain
And its eternity of white clouds—

And that I should ask no more questions